my reclaimed blessing journal

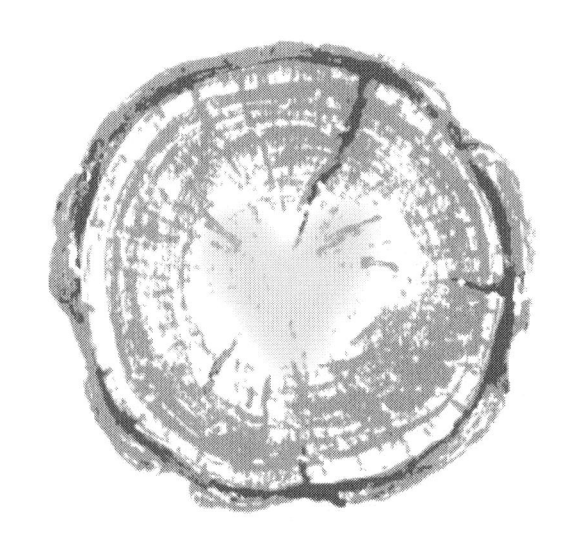

My Reclaimed Blessing Journal

By **Stephanie Broersma**
ISBN: 978-179-138-3138

My Reclaimed Blessing Journal, by Stephanie Broersma (August 8,1980); copyright © 2018; published by Reclaimed Ministry. International Secured Book Number 978-179-138-3138. All rights reserved. No part of this book may be reproduced or transmitted in any form or by any means, electronic or mechanical, including photocopying, recording or by any information storage and retrieval system, in any manner whatsoever, without prior written permission of the Author, except in the case of brief quotations in critical articles and reviews.
All Scriptures are taken from Holy Bible, New International Version (NIV); copyright © 1973, 1978, 1984, 2011 by Biblica, Inc.; used by permission; all rights reserved worldwide.

Cover Design by Lisa DenBleyker, Lynden, WA and Chad Williams, Lynden, WA. Printed in the United States. For more information, contact:
Reclaimed Ministry Stephanie Broersma
P.O. Box 569
Lynden, Washington, 98264 United States of America

To learn more about Reclaimed Ministry and related materials, visit:
www.reclaimedandwhole.com
@reclaimedministry

The purpose of this journal is to record your thoughts as you process the Reclaimed 30 Day Devotional or as you work your way through the Reclaimed Small Group.
Ask God to reveal the areas in your heart that
He is asking you to stretch, grow and to be challenged in as you continue to navigate your journey.
Pray for your eyes to be opened in order to see all that God has put in your path to encourage you, strengthen, and give you the God wink needed for the day.
Part of healing is being able to look back and see the prayer requests answered - such a faith booster to see God actively working in your life.
Celebrate the blessings, write them down, and give God all the glory in your story!

> "Come and listen, all you who fear God; let me tell you what he has done for me."
> Psalm 66:16

{ *What are your two blessings for today?* }

Today I am Thankful for...

"To bestow on them a crown of beauty instead of ashes, the oil of gladness instead of mourning, and a garment of praise instead of a spirit of despair. They will be called oaks of righteousness.
Instead of their shame my people will receive a double portion, and instead of disgrace they will rejoice in their inheritance; and so they will inherit a double portion in their land, and
everlasting joy will be theirs."
Isaiah 61:3,7

Count Your Blessings... Name them One by One

1.
2.
3.
4.
5.
6.
7.
8.
9.
10.
11.
12.
13.
14.
15.
16.
17.
18.
19.
20.
21.
22.
23.
24.
25.

"Blessed are the peacemakers, for they will be called children of God. Blessed are those who are persecuted because of righteousness, for theirs is the kingdom of heaven. Blessed are you when people insult you, persecute you and falsely say all kinds of evil against you because of me."
Matthew 5:9-11

{ What are your two blessings for today? }

Remind yourself of ways God has never left you.
"It is the Lord who goes before you. He will be with you; He will not leave you or forsake you.
Do not fear or be dismayed."
Deuteronomy 31:8

_____
_____
_____
_____
_____
_____
_____
_____
_____
_____
_____
_____
_____
_____
_____
_____
_____
_____
_____
_____

"When we remember His awesomeness, our challenges look smaller in comparison to His greatness. Praise has great power in fighting spiritual battles"
Taking Care of the "Me" In Mommy
by Lisa Whelchel

"When times are good, be happy; but when times are bad, consider: God has made the one as well as the other."
Ecclesiastes 7:14

What is God teaching you today?

What is God calling you to do today?

How is God blessing you with today?

"The way we go after opportunities reveals what we're made of. The dew of blessing; the critical part of a Christian's gaze recognizing the blessings and goodness in a situation that also function to reveal the human heart."
– David Powlison

"He will wipe every tear from their eyes. There will be no more death or mourning or crying or pain, for the old order of things has passed away."
Revelation 21:4

1.
2.
3.
4.
5.
6.
7.
8.
9.
10.
11.
12.
13.
14.
15.
16.
17.
18.
19.
20.
21.
22.
23.
24.
25.

"Redeemed women of God have tender merciful hearts, backbones of steel, and hands that are prepared for the fight."
— Stasi Eldredge

{ What are your two blessings for today? }

"May these words of my mouth and the meditation of my heart, be pleasing in your sight, Lord,
my Rock, and my Redeemer."
Psalm 19:14

Write down 20 things you are thankful for in your home.

1.
2.
3.
4.
5.
6.
7.
8.
9.
10.
11.
12.
13.
14.
15.
16.
17.
18.
19.
20.

"Rejoice in the Lord always, I will say it again: Rejoice! Let your gentleness be evident to all. The Lord is near. Do not be anxious about anything, but in everything by prayer and petition, with thanksgiving, present your requests to God. And the peace of God, which transcends all understanding, will guard your hearts and your minds in Christ Jesus."
Philippians 4:4-7

> "But the fruit of the Spirit is love, joy, peace, forbearance, kindness, goodness, faithfulness, gentleness, and self control."
> Galatians 5:22

"Be joyful in hope, patient in affliction,
faithful in prayer."
Romans 12:12

{ What are your two blessings for today? }

"Consider it pure joy, my brothers and sisters, whenever you face trials of many kinds, because you know that the testing of your faith produces perseverance."
James 1:2-3

> "Therefore my heart is glad and my tongue rejoices;
> my body will also rest secure."
> Psalm 16:9

{ What are your two blessings for today? }

> "My lips will shout for joy, when I sing praise to you - I whom you have delivered."
> Psalm 71:23

"Those who sow with tears, will reap with songs of joy."
Psalm 126:5

"Fear & doubt are conquered by a faith that rejoices. And faith can rejoice because the promises of God are as certain as God Himself."
-Kay Arthur

My cup overflows with blessings.
Psalm 23:5

{ *What are your two blessings for today?* }

{ *thankful . grateful . blessed* }

{ eucharistos: } *to be thankful*

{ hallelujah }

{ What are your two blessings for today? }

Thank you Jesus for meeting all my needs today…

Definition of grateful

1. a: appreciative of benefits received: expressing gratitude grateful thanks
2. a: affording pleasure or contentment: pleasing: pleasing by reason of comfort supplied or discomfort alleviated

{ Bless the Lord oh my soul! }

The root of JOY is gratefulness.

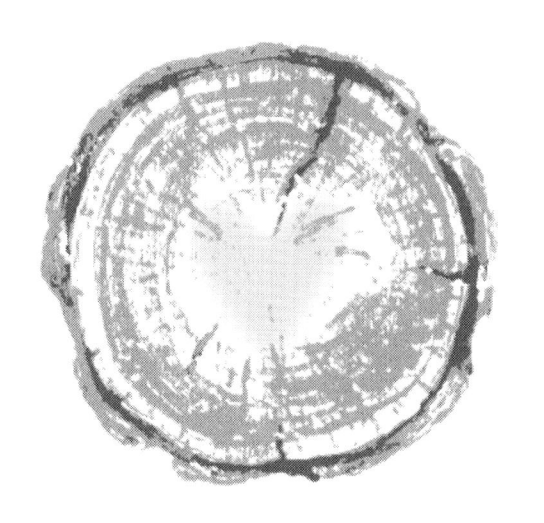

For more information, contact:

Reclaimed Ministry

Stephanie Broersma
P.O. Box 569
Lynden, Washington, 98264
United States of America

www.reclaimedandwhole.com
@reclaimedministry

20387812R00029

Made in the USA
San Bernardino, CA
05 January 2019